AF445744

Table of Contents

About The Author

Shuchi Mishra has been teaching English in an international school for more than 4 years. She's the wife of a software engineer and the mother of a young boy but she's also been a piano player and a singer.

She is an energetic, committed and fully-qualified English teacher who has a passion for teaching and also holds a Master's degree (MA) and an undergraduate degree (BA) in English Language and Literature from the University of Lucknow. She is an award winning Parenting and Leadership expert who specializes in helping parents to raise happy, confident and responsible children in this digital age. She is also the author of "_You Will Always Be An Employee: A short story about office politics_".

Dedication

For Ahan, who is the source of much pleasure and fulfilment in our lives.

INTRODUCTION

Our world is financed driven. As much as we eat and live, some paper, coin or some other form of money has to change hands. It will be unimaginable to think that we can survive without the presence of that lucre. Economies of nations are tied to the amount of wealth generated or made available in the hands of her countrymen. A nation is considered prosperous once there is a large increase in the monetary spending power of her citizens. The opposite is the case when there is less of monetary spending power.

In a world where most are poor, crave for the opportunity to raise money and increase the standard of living is rife. The average man wants to live in the car, home, and society of his beat dreams. However just a few manage to break the divide because they lack the proper parenting during childhood.

The huge gap between the haves and the have not is increasing almost every day. Those who manage to break off from the latter to the former have been well fortified with knowledge right from the early stage. They grappled with their difference and determined that they would break the divide and they have. But they had something to help propel that aspiration, they had knowledge.

The popular saying that the rich will continue to get richer while the poor will increasingly get poorer isn't far from the truth. This is because those who have attained the rich height increasing think of having more. They think of the future today and position their kid's right from their childhood to be creative and business-like in their approach to any opportunity in life. They train their wards to see opportunity and back them up with the financial capacity to see that opportunity become reality.

The rich teach their children independence from their children helping them understand the power of money and the acts of entrepreneurship. The poor are often the employees, always thinking of how to raise money that never comes because often they never get enough. Their kids often show the same dependency attributes. The cycle thus continues generations and generations after.

I want to thank you and congratulate you for downloading the book, "smart parenting". This book contains proven steps and strategies on how to parent your child through the child.

Parenting with Love and Logic puts the fun into parenting. The time of early childhood development is a really important period when a mother or a father should form a secure relationship with their child, and that is during the first two years of life. That period appears to be critical to the child's social and emotional development. Early childhood is the period in your child's life which need your special attention.This book will help you to manage parenting with love and logic.

If you want to do smart parenting for your smart kids, this book is for you.The relationship between a parent and a child is among the most significant in a person's life. As one of the earliest connections a child has, the parental relationship sets the bar for everyone thereafter. In this book, you will learn how to adapt your parent-child relationship with time. This book will also teach how to talk to your child so that your child can listen you and start talking.

All you need to do is after reading this eBook make sure you take action and you will be building a solid foundation for the success of your children.

This book is inspired base on the fact that many parents make their children their retirement plan. Forgetting the major development stage of a child ("childhood" which comes but once) giving them proper parenting to prepare them for a successful future. Thanks again for downloading this book, I hope you enjoy it.

CHAPTER ONE

Parenting

From talking and reading to infants to making values clear (best done in conversations around the dinner table), parents exert enormous influence over their children's development. They are, however, not the only influences, especially after children enter school. It is especially important that parents give children a good start, but it's also important for parents to recognize that kids come into the world with their own temperaments, and it is the parents' job to provide an interface with the world that eventually prepares a child for complete independence. In a rapidly changing world, parenting seems subject to fads and changing styles, and parenting in some ways has become a competitive sport.

But the needs of child development as delineated by science remain relatively stable. There is such a thing as over parenting, and aiming for perfection in parenting might be a fool's mission. Too much parenting cripples children as they move into adulthood and renders them unable to cope with the merest setbacks. There is also such a thing as too-little parenting, and research establishes that lack of parental engagement often leads to poor behavioral outcomes in children, in part because it encourages the young to be too reliant on peer culture. Ironically, harsh or authoritarian styles of parenting can have the same effect.

Basic Parenting Styles

Parenting is something that usually comes naturally to people. There are no hard fast how to manuals or rules to parenting. People generally just learn as they go. Most things are just second nature, like feeding, clothing and generally caring for a child. However, as a child grows and other children are born, parenting becomes more than simply handling the child's everyday needs. Sometimes parents feel they need some help in deciding the best way to parent their children.

There have been many people who have spoken out about parenting and offered advice and assistance to parents in need. Parenting styles are an example of something a parent can do to help them with their parenting. A parenting style is basically a way to describe how a parent parents their child or children. There are 3 basic types of parenting styles.

Some authorities on the subject of parenting will argue that there are many different variations of parenting styles, but they all go back to the three basic parenting styles. Those three styles are authoritarian, permissive and democratic.

Authoritarian Parenting Style

Most parents only want the best for their children. However, there are instances when parents can be highly demanding and less responsive to their children's needs, interests, and desires. Parenting is seen as a typology, in which specific practices are held insignificant compared with the general practices on how parents deal with their children.

Experts describe authoritarian parenting as a style that is based on obedience without question. In families adopting authoritarian parenting, parents most often enforce stringent rules, where punishment is confused for discipline. Authoritarian parenting holds high regard for achievement, leaving children with no room to make mistakes. Often, this style of parenting is devoid of love and affection that are, in fact, very crucial in the psychological and emotional development of young children.

Parents might not recognize it, but authoritarian parenting can lead to future problems when it comes to the relationship between children and parents. Children of authoritarian parents are prone to committing rebellious acts, as their way of asserting their individuality and finding their niche in the society.

Another downside to this style of parenting is that children have the tendency to open their problems to other people due to fear of their parents, which is not a healthy parent-child relationship. Out of the parents' desire for achievement and ensuring that their children turn out to be successful adults, they fail on the opportunity to provide guidance when the children most need it. Instead, they enforce black and white rules that often neglect the children's chance to grow and learn from mistakes. In turn, this leads to confusion that significantly damages a child's self-esteem as well as social competence.

Children from authoritarian families can perform moderately in school, which is a stark contrast to how their parents aim for them, although they may have no involvement in problematic behavior in societies. Yet, children from these families have a higher degree of depression, partly because they cannot express their own thoughts and interests to their parents, consequently stifling their intellectual growth.

Discipline in authoritarian parenting tends to be harsh and does not quantify the wrongdoing. Eventually, parents are baffled as to what method of discipline to impose when spanking no longer works. In some families, spanking can lead to abuse which correlates to the low self-esteem and poor social skills of children.

Many experts have discouraged parents to use authoritarian parenting style due to its proven detrimental effects on a child's well-being. Instead, psychologists advocate a more democratic parenting style that fosters parent-child relationship but ensures that children grow to be responsible and loving individuals.

The authoritarian parenting style is based on control. With this style of parenting, the parent retains complete control at all times. Under this style of parenting, there are strict rules and schedules. The parents rule the children with an iron fist. There is no exception to the rules and punishment is given in a very orderly and prompt fashion when it is needed. The downside of an authoritarian parenting style is that it usually does not allow for a lot of affection or warmth. Since children raised with this parenting style are usually not allowed to think freely or make decisions on their own they often grow up to have problems with thinking for themselves.

Permissive Parenting Style

Bringing up kids is never easy. In fact, it is one of the most challenging tasks a parent can have. There are several parenting styles that parents use to bring up their kids, and using just one style is not the best way to make your child a responsible and morally upright person.

One style of parenting that has been often criticized is the permissive parenting style wherein the parents tend to be overindulgent when bringing up their child. In this style of parenting, parents tend to be highly attentive to the needs of the child and give him or her everything without making them work for it. Here the kids are not corrected or taught to behave in the correct manner. This style of parenting is the exact opposite of the authoritative parenting style where the parents are too strict and do not give children the space to be kids.

Parents tend to give all their love to the kids and do not check them when their behavior is wrong. The kids, in turn, do not have to follow any rules and cannot look up at their parents to guide them. This can leave the kids bewildered and confused. This style of parenting believes that kids ought to make their own choices, be it right or wrong. Hence, their wrong behavior is not punished or corrected.

Due to permissive parenting, kids tend to get spoilt and are used to getting their own way. They will not be able to distinguish right from wrong and are never prepared to handle disappointments and rejections that will come their way later on in life. Such kids are the ones who throw tantrums when their demands are not met. It has been seen that using this parenting style with teenagers can lead the adolescents towards anti-social behavior like smoking, drug abuse, and shoplifting.

At the same time, permissive parenting is ideal for kids who are shy and introverts. This allows them sufficient space to grow as individuals and blossom. On the other hand, this kind of parenting is the wrong style for kids who are difficult to handle or who are rebellious in nature.

Parents that use this parenting style feel that their children need to be free thinkers and be able to explore the world and learn for themselves without being held down by rules and strict structure. There is often a lot of affection and warmth with this parenting styles. The downside though, is that children do not learn that rules are sometimes necessary. They learn that no matter what they do - right or wrong- that they will not be punished. This can lead to a lifelong rebellion against any type of rule or structure.

Democratic Parenting Style

There are no hard and fast rules of how you should discipline your child. Though parenting skills are equipped with all parents automatically, the level of the effect varies according to the parenting styles applied by the parents.

The democratic parenting style is a mixture of the authoritarian and permissive parenting styles. A democratic parent will set rules that are necessary and enforce them, but they will also take each situation as it comes. Punishment is usually discussed with the child. Democratic parents are most interested in making sure their children understand why rules are in place and why some behavior is unacceptable. Democratic parenting is about letting children know when they do well and when they do bad making sure they understand why it is wrong. It is a style of parenting where everyone - parents and children- work together. Children will usually grow up to respect their parents and to be able to handle conflicts and problems in a reasonable manner.

Each parenting style has its pros and cons, obviously, with the authoritarian parenting style, the children are going to be very respectful and very well behaved. The parents will have very little chaos and they will have a low-stress level. With the permissive parenting style, the parent is free to do whatever they want because they are not constantly policing the children. The family simply does their own thing, which can often lead to a lot of separation over time as everyone develops their own life apart from the family. The democratic parent in style requires a lot of work. Parents must constantly be talking with and dealing with their children in order to keep everyone involved in the family.

Nobody ever claimed parenting was easy. There really is no right or wrong to parent as long as children are cared for, happy and healthy. Parents can choose for themselves how they want to parent their children. Some parents simply fall into a parenting style that seems to fit their own lives and their own beliefs. Others make a conscious effort to maintain a parenting style. However, a parent chooses their parent style, it is fine as long as it works for them and their children are taken care of.

CHILDHOOD

Childhood is a period of life when one is a child. It passes so quickly but brings so many memories until one dies. That is, it is such a period of life when one passes their life from two to twelve years of their beginning age. The period between 2-6 years is called early childhood and from 6-12 is called childhood.

During childhood, a child is much more creative and inquisitive. They have a power of mixing in a group and making friends. The child wants to experience everything by doing it. Children always like to follow the truth. They tell everything that they see or listen or do. Looking at the activities of a child, one can easily guess what the child will become in the future.

A child shows its characteristic features in childhood. Therefore childhood is the foundation of manhood that is a child is the father of the man. Children have a good appetite for love, sympathy, and response to their queries. We must not oversee their activities or questions. They should be treated as a good companion so that they never hesitate to ask anything to elders. We shouldn't forget that they are very imitative, creative, quarrelsome, sloppy and stubborn.

What comes to your mind when you think about childhood? Here's what comes to mine. Learning to ride a bike. Climbing trees. The pebbles on Cromer beach. Clapping games. Skipping games. Marbles. Conkers. Stealing fistfuls of blackjacks from the village shop. Great-aunts with spiky chins. One whole summer holiday spent acting out Swallows and Amazons. Chinese burns. Camping in the airing cupboard. Pan's People. Doctors and nurses. Crying in math's lessons. Hating all math's teachers. Waiting hours and hours and hours for Sunday lunch to be ready, and then getting served last. Lying in bed late at night, wondering if the voices downstairs were the television or my parents arguing.

It's easy to over-simplify the idea of childhood, and the children who inhabit that phase of life; tempting to tidy it up retrospectively into all-good or all bad. But allow the mind to roam freely for a moment around "the great cathedral space" of childhood, as Virginia Woolf called it, and what one retrieves are very varied memories.

In our idealized images of childhood, it's the physical and spiritual purity of the young that comes to the fore. Adults are benign, shadowy figures, if not entirely absent, then firmly in the background. We think (inevitably) of that saccharine Pears soap child, all peachy cheeks, and soft, gold curls, or of children in parks or on beaches, bright points of energy, absorbed in the sheer pleasure of being young.

CHILDHOOD MEMORIES

What are your best childhood memories? Is it of fun and games in school? Is it of loving times with Mom and Dad? Memories have great power over us. Memories of good times can sustain us throughout our lives, especially during periods of great turmoil. Unhappy memories, too, have a strong hold on our emotions and actions long after the event.

Childhood memories are the first memories we make. They can be like pleasant dreams which bring a smile to our face or nightmares from which we wish we could awaken. As parents, we can influence the type of memories our children will have of their childhood years. We can fill their memories with laughter, loving words and family togetherness. Or we can fill it with constant admonitions, criticisms and frequent quarrels.

We can never be sure of what kind of memories we will remember. Which events will stand out? Think of your strongest memories. Is it on major occasions like vacations and birthdays? Or is it of the smallest incidents - a conversation, shared laughter, a goodnight kiss? Knowing that memories can be formed at any time, we must be more aware of what happens during everyday interactions. Your child's childhood memories will likely be made of the quiet moments when you are enjoying each other's company or the quarrels you had.

The school takes up a large bulk of the childhood years. When children start school, it is all too easy for parents to get caught up in the competition for grades. In an effort to make sure our children do not fall behind their peers, we nag them to do their homework, nag them to stop playing so much and maybe send them for tons of enrichment classes. What we often forget to do though is take the time to listen to them; to discuss current affairs so they understand what is going on in the community, or to just let them know that you value them beyond their grades in school.

Yes, school and grades are important. But what is more crucial is that your children enjoy their childhood. We can learn academic subjects throughout our life. We only have a few short years to enjoy our childhood. Your children's childhood memories should be of more than just studying, studying and more studying. They should remember the parties they had; the silly, childish fun they had with their friends or the loving family outings they enjoyed with cousins, aunts, and uncles.

In school, our children have to learn to face myriad situations. They may face strict teachers, indifferent teachers, bullies, fair-weather friends and a competitive learning environment. How they cope and what kind of memories they form depends on their attitude towards their situation. If they view it as a challenge which they are capable of overcoming, then they will have happy childhood memories of school. If they see it as insurmountable difficulties, then they will form nightmarish childhood memories which they hate to remember.

We can help them develop the right attitude so they form happy childhood memories. Being aware of our influence is half the battle won. Take the time to make sure your child has wonderful childhood memories.

CHILDHOOD EDUCATION

Early childhood education typically pertains to the education of children who range in age from babies to kindergarten age. This does not start and end inside the classroom. Early childhood training is debatably the most crucial phase of educational development as it is from this cornerstone that future development and learning happen. High-quality programs need to incorporate teaching in reading capabilities, motor skills, and vocabulary and communication abilities. This will create substantial benefits in children's understanding and development. Early youth training has gotten much more attention each year due to the outcomes of research which continually document that a child will become a more successful student in the course of his school years and in higher education if they have been positively impacted in the primary grades.

Preschool children must be provided early reading and writing, recognition and involvement to be able to perform better through the later years. Preschool Teachers perform an essential part during the early childhood development because they're a part of the child's initial experience of learning inside a classroom environment. Preschool training also was significantly found as a factor assisting families to balance child rearing and work duties. Preschool enrollment has rapidly elevated throughout the nation within the last many decades. Directors of preschool's state they are uncertain how to supply parenting details considering that attendance is commonly surprisingly low at planned programs on child development and parenting. A preschool education that has a properly preserved atmosphere and properly educated teachers that have ideas knowledge and conceptions to carry out beneficial training to make kids a good human being is the perfect spot for all parents.

The development of behavior, values, and long-term habits requires a relationship involving you, the early childhood instructor, as well as the families of your young ones. Child Development levels are encased in a multitude of places. Motor development means adjustments in a child's movement capabilities; motor learning will be the abilities obtained from practice and experience. Child development and involved efforts to improve the quality and pace of the child's ability acquisition via early childhood schooling involve the reality that understanding basic abilities early on in life results in a far better understanding of complicated skills in the future. Concentrated growth and development of earlier childhood training programs are now in demand. The overall disposition would be that the age-scope of beginning childhood education and learning needs to be expanded from preschool and pre-primary age groups to all young children from birth.

The time prior to a young child gets to kindergarten are the most crucial in their life to impact learning. From numerous years of research and practice, it is understood that every young child through newborns, toddlers and preschoolers are essentially different than older kids and have to be educated in fundamentally different methods. More than twenty years of numerous studies have identified that high quality early in childhood education is: Holistic; Nurturing; Constant; Hands-On; Simulative; Exploratory; and Combines involved learning throughout the curriculum. For quite some time, information continues to be amassing about the need for committing to young -- very young -- minds and the potential risk of depending on common K-12 education models to change kids into wholesome, successful grownups. The first years of a child's existence will be the most significant within their development. The early years of a child's life have a very considerable effect on human brain development, social-emotional intelligence, and personal identification.

Parents, caretakers, neighbors and preschool educators perform a crucial role during the early years of a child's education. Most mothers and fathers tend to be naturally concerned with the caliber of the early childhood education programs accessible to them. Mothers and fathers, the majority of whom are employed, have to know that their small children not merely are learning but additionally are being properly cared for throughout the working day. Parents will help make their child's initial experience successful by examining their own thoughts and expectations, and by considering how they may strengthen skills that the child is required to have at school. Parents are their kid's very first teachers and definitely will proceed all through life to be instructors for their kids.

Due to the fact of the high demand for finding inexpensive, high-quality education for young children within their most significant early years of learning, expenses have increased significantly. Teachers are in high demand for this particular field, but education as a parent or guardian is vital to assisting kids to develop correctly. Moms and Dads are now able to give their children top quality early learning skills from home at an extremely small cost. The same Early Learning Academy which is used all through schools and daycare's by teachers, and organizations nationwide can now be accessed on the internet. The cost of a full year from home is lower than the expense of one week of sending a child to educational centers, day-cares, and so on. This can also be accessed on a monthly basis for under ten dollars a month, and is recognized, and utilized by educational facilities and learning centers through the entire nation.

The Concept of Childhood Education

The concept of early childhood education typically applies to the pre-elementary school years when parents are interested in putting their children in a kindergarten or preschool program. Many parents currently believe that the earlier a child's education gets started, the more successful they are going to be later on in life. Today, parents are fortunate to have a number of options at their disposal besides public preschool including the Head Start, Montessori, Reggio Emilia, and Waldorf programs.

Public preschool

The public preschool form of early childhood education has gained in popularity in recent decades throughout the US and are typically state-funded. These programs were primarily designed for low-income families and will provide an education to any child residing in that particular school district. The availability will vary from one state to the next and then from district to district.

Head Start

Federal money is the funding source for the many Head Start programs located throughout the US. These are geared to those families who have children under 5 years of age and who are at a lower level of income. There are also what are referred to as Early Head Start programs that focus on children who are between zero and three years of age as well as pregnant women. Additionally, children who have medical or psychological conditions and are receiving public assistance are usually eligible for a Head Start program.

Montessori Schools

These early childhood education programs focus on those children that are between three and six years of age. Some of them even feature toddler-oriented programs while others offer programs for infants. Children in these programs experience a hands-on learning experience as they are directed through a series of educational materials. The teachers of these facilities are typically referred to as "directresses" since they direct children through specific activities instead of just teaching them in standard fashion.

Reggio Emilia approach

As this name would seem to imply, this early childhood education program has Italian roots just like the Montessori schools. In the Reggio Emilia approach, the learning process is collaborated by the children, parents, and teachers in the school. If the child shows an interest in a particular activity, they will be provided with ample opportunities to learn a curriculum that feeds that particular interest. Parents are encouraged to participate in the child's curriculum and are given educational materials to help them do so.

Waldorf Early Childhood Program

In these early childhood education programs, the teacher engages in artistic, domestic, and practical activities and encourages the children in their class to imitate them. The teacher also encourages them to use their imagination during dramatic play and storytelling. The toys that are used in Waldorf programs are manufactured using only natural materials.

Children will also bring nature items that they are interested in so they can explore them and play with them in class. The Waldorf curriculum is based on three child development age groups - birth to age 7, 7 years to 14 years, and 14 years to 18 years of age.

Imparting Early Childhood Education

One way to ensure that your child stays on track in school is to start as early as possible with early childhood education. There are many ways that a child can learn before they enter school. When you take the time to think about it, everything and everywhere can be a part of a lesson. For example, at three years old a trip to the grocery store can help establish critical thinking techniques that your child can use later on in school; like the process of elimination. You may not buy a product because it is too high or it has something in it that you or your child is allergic to. This process of elimination will help your child see how to eliminate all selections and choose the right one.

Early childhood education is also available on television for preschoolers. Not every program or cartoon for a child is educational so you need to find a program that teaches and enhances early childhood education. Watch a few of the episodes to determine how they mix fun with early childhood education. It may be a funny cartoon or show or it could be a serious episode with a good ending.

Early childhood education can be found in children's books. Many books focus on preschool ages and can help strengthen the important details to help prepare them for school. You can purchase books on patterns, colors, numbers, and letters. Books start out with pictures and textures that allow you to feel the words such as "fur". These books keep the child's mind occupied while teaching a lesson at the same time. Books come in a variety of color with pictures that relate to the story and can teach the child in a way that they can learn. The concept of the story is funny, interesting, exciting, or serious.

When early childhood is worked with from the beginning, it helps prepare a child for the start of school. Some children start as early as three in a preschool program while others start when they turn five. Most three-year-old programs will focus on creative learning that is fun in order for the child to remember what they see and hear and process the information so they can use it when they start attending school daily.

Early childhood education is exciting with endless possibilities. It can also bring a smile to a parent when you see how your child takes the information and processes it. Their childhood educational tools should be offered to a child at all times. When they are developmentally ready for them they will pick them up and begin to study them. As your child grows so does the need for more up-to-date books that will challenge the mind and stimulate growth and development.

CHAPTER TWO

PARENTING POWER

President Obama has a cradle-to-career plan to reform USA's schools. He also is calling on parents to take responsibility for their child's success. His vision includes the belief that all children can and will succeed, and that parents are the bridge to this success. You as the parent, guardian or caregiver can help your child by connecting with his or her school to find out what's needed to ensure success and how you can help reach that goal. Studies of successful schools report that parent involvement is a major factor in their outcomes, including closing the achievement gap between various groups of students. With his vision, the president is asking that you make education a priority and a legacy for your family.

Are there areas in your relationship with the children in your life where you feel powerless to change the situation? Times when "the kids" seem out of control and no matter what you've done to get them to change, they keep being uncooperative.

For whatever comfort this is you are not alone. Most parents, teachers, and grandparents struggle with some aspect of their relationship with children. Children who ignore your requests to pick up their toys or to come to the dinner table on time. Children who scream when you tell them "No."

The sad part of these stories is we adults too often persist in doing the same things over and over to solve these challenges even though our strategies don't produce the results we want. Parents and teachers frequently tell me the same list of strategies they have tried--bribes, threats, punishment, reasoning, explaining--all of which do not create the desired long-term results.

The commonality in all of these approaches is they are intended to get the child to change her behavior. You unconsciously reason, "If only my child would act the way I want, everything would be all right." You keep hoping you can threaten, cajole, reason, bribe, or punish your child for compliance.

Many of you have heard this before. There is only one person whose behavior you can change, and it is your own. Yet how much time do you devote to trying to get your child to change? Or your boss or your spouse or your parents? We waste a lot of our time, energy and power trying to get others to change. If we put that same attention, power, and energy into our own change, we might actually get the results we want.

The good news is your child will change her behavior in response to your changed behavior. It can seem to work like magic.

Changing your own behavior can feel difficult. Doing new things requires courage, awareness, and lots of self-love. Your new behavior feels unfamiliar and uncomfortable, and you don't know what's going to happen when you do it consistently.

Here are a couple of suggestions to get you started.

- Determine which situations are not working for you. You'll discover some things are more important to you than others. Pay attention to your highest priorities first.

- Choose one thing you will do differently to improve your own behavior and choices in the situation. Focus on this new behavior daily so you can successfully follow through.

- Observe the results in how you feel and how your child/student acts. Are you feeling better about the situation? How is your child responding?

When you use the power you have, you can create a wonderful connection with your child and have a lot of fun. Parenting becomes so much easier, and your child flourishes as an emotionally healthy person.

USING PARENTING POWER WISELY

As mentioned in a previously, Parent Power is the authority given to us to guide our children towards acceptable behavior. It is a neutral power that is automatically given and, when used effectively, can help us raise resilient kids while building a strong, positive relationship with them.

Gaining our children's compliance is not always an easy thing to do which is why we need our power to back up our words when they refuse to listen. Our goal with our kids is to teach them how to think for themselves and understand why what we tell them to do is necessary, rather than have them blindly follow our direction.

In the end, we want to have taught our kids our version of right versus wrong created a strong, loving relationship with them so they want to be part of our lives, and built up mutual respect so they will work with us during those tumultuous teenage years.

Five ideas for using Parenting power wisely:

Provide clear expectations, enforcement, and follow-through. Kids crave structure. They like to know what is expected of them and what the potential consequence will be for breaking that rule. Just like us, they feel an injustice has been done when they are not told of expectations and then get in trouble for breaking a rule. Be clear about your rules, enforce them consistently and do your best to follow-through on the planned consequence.

Allow choices. People like to be allowed to make their own decisions - although some will oppose it on occasion. People who resist choices usually have something else going on for the - fear of making a bad decision, challenges with self-regulation, etc. Allowing our kids to make choices and teaching them how to make good ones is an important part of helping them develop.

Guide rather than a boss. Notice the kind of language that you use and when possible choose words that suggest an action rather than ordering it. For example, "Pick up your jacket" becomes "Your jacket belongs on a hook." Depending on your child's personality this can make the difference between regular fights and voluntary compliance. When we boss people around we are using our power and frivolous use of our power does not build respect. Save the bossing for moments when there really is no choice, and practice using positive communication the rest of the time.

Choose your battles carefully. There are a lot of things to correct, advice on, or lecture our kids about and if we do them all we cannot possibly build a positive relationship with them. Remember your kids will do things differently from you and will have their own perspective about what is right or wrong in many situations. Anytime you have to fight to get your way, you are not teaching, but forcing compliance.

Be creative. Rather than going on automatic and pulling out habitual parenting tools (spanking, grounding, yelling, time-out...) force yourself to think creatively about the situation. Parenting is not a task to do on auto-pilot and yet so often that is what we do. When our kids are babies most of us experiment to figure out how to stop them fussing. As our kids grow and start pushing our buttons we often stop thinking and start reacting. When we force ourselves to come up with a new idea to try we are developing our own brain pathways along with those of our child.

The less you use your power muscle and the more you practice using positive parenting strategies, the more you will benefit when your kids reach that rebellious, teenager stage. We all need to use our power sometimes, we just need to be sure we don't get lazy and start using it to get our way all of the time. The choice is ours... we have the power to make a difference!

BE YOUR CHILD'S ROLE MODEL FOR SUCCESS

How can you accomplish this? By adopting the following principles and taking the steps indicated for each age group, you will be able to help your child learn at each step of the way and ensure success in school and in life.

Be responsible.

Accept your role as the parent and make education a priority in your home.

Be committed.

Once you have begun to work with your child, continue doing so throughout the year.

Be positive.

Praise goes a long way with children, especially with those who struggle in school.

Provide positive feedback.

Be patient. Show your child that you care about your commitment and encouragement.

Be attentive.

Stop your child immediately when bad behavior appears. Show him or her what to do and provide an opportunity to do it correctly. Discipline should be appropriate and consistent.

Be precise.

Provide clear and direct instructions.

Be mindful of mistakes.

Record your child's performance. Look over all the work your child brings home from school and keep it in a folder. Help him or her correct any errors.

Be results-oriented.

Gather information on how your child is performing in school. Keep notes of conferences with teachers, request progress reports and carefully read report cards and achievement test results. Ask questions about these results.

Be diligent.

Work from the beginning to the end of the year with your child and the teacher.

Be innovative.

Keep learning lively and dynamic.

BE There.

Just be there for your child–to answer questions, to listen, to give advice, to encourage and to speak positively about his or her life. Be there to support your child whenever needed.

Ensure That Your Child Is Ready to Learn

You also can be part of your child's educational experience by teaching and reinforcing the skills your child needs and enhancing those taught in the classroom. Using the following checklists, you can help your child be a successful student from preschool through high school

Make sure your child's: a Physical needs are met with a healthy diet, enough sleep and rest, exercise and good medical care; a Social and emotional needs are met. A Confidence, independence, and cooperation skills are built; a Discipline is appropriate and consistent. a Play is stimulating; a Questions are answered; a Caregiver or preschool teacher has books to read to your child and does read to your child every day, and a Day is filled with different learning activities.

Preschool is a great opportunity for your little one to learn. There are a lot of kids to interact with, for starters, which will essentially help your child learn social skills that will be very important when he grows up. However, the sheer number of new faces to see and meet can be overwhelming at first. Here are some things you can do to ensure that your child is ready for preschool.

Talk to your child - even before school starts, talk to your child about preschool. Tell him why he needs to go and what can he expect. Explain to him that your home and the preschool will have similarities so there's no need to be afraid. Helping a kid understand what's happening will help prevent tantrums on the first day of school so he can actually go to school on that day without throwing a fit.

Do a show-and-tell - it will help your child ease into the situation if you bring him around to the preschool before he starts. The entrance alone can be overwhelming to a child since it is unfamiliar territory, but letting him get used to it will help calm him down. Letting your kid warm up to the preschool will also give you time to get to know his teacher and the common activities and routines that they have.

Don't be nervous yourself - kids are like sponges absorbing everything around them and this includes your anxiety. They will sense that you don't want to leave them at school so they won't feel secure enough to stay there as well. Assure yourself that it's going to be alright. Kids go to preschools all over the world and their playground memories will be one of the best they may have.

Is your child really ready? All the best kinds of preparations for preschool will be for naught if your kid is not ready to go to school at all. Some of the things you can watch out for to consider if your kid is ready to head to preschool includes: the ability to communicate verbally, how he responds to discipline, his physical ability to be out there with other kids, jumping, climbing, and playing around, and how he is when you are not around. If your kid is leaning towards the positive end of these signs then he may be ready to go to preschool.

Ready Your Child for Reading

It's never too soon to start your child on the path to reading. Simply talking to your infant and toddler helps her develop the vocabulary she will need as she enters school and begins to read. As you point to and name objects, she will begin to understand the meaning of words, and will eventually begin to incorporate those words into his vocabulary.

The U.S. Department of Education recommends beginning to read to your baby when she is six months old. According to their 2003 report, "Hearing words over and over helps her become familiar with them. Reading to your baby is one of the best ways to help her learn."

In that same report, the Department of Education also recommends that parents reach out to groups that can:

Help you find age-appropriate books to use at home with your child; Show you creative ways to use books with your child and other tips to help her learn; and Provide year-round children's reading and educational activities.

A child's love for reading grows when the words on the page come to life through experiences shared as a family. For example, after reading Eric Carle's Ten Little Rubber Ducks to your toddler, you can learn all about real ducks, make ocean snacks, or go on a family outing and feed the ducks at a nearby pond.

In order to help your child get ready to read, the Department of Education also recommends:

Using sounds, songs, gestures, and words that rhyme to help your baby learn about language and its many uses. Pointing out the printed words in your home and other places you take your child, such as the grocery store. Spending as much time listening to your child as you do talking to her. Taking children's books and writing materials with you whenever you leave home. This gives your child fun activities to entertain and occupy her while traveling and running errands.

Creating a quiet, special place in your home for your child to read, write, and draw.

Keeping books and other reading materials where your child can easily reach them. Having her own bookshelf or small bookcase will not only make her feel special but will also communicate to her that reading is special.

Reading books, newspapers, and magazines yourself, so that your child can see that reading is important.

Limiting the amount and type of television you and your child watch. The best thing you do to ensure that your child will grow up reading well and love to read is to read to her every day. The time you spend reading together will create a special bond between the two of you and will open the doors for a dialogue that will continue throughout the more trying years of adolescence. The Department of Education suggests that, when you're reading, you discuss new words. As an example, they suggest that you say, "This big house is called a palace. Who do you think lives in a palace?" Likewise, they suggest taking time to ask about the pictures and what your child thinks is happening in the story.

The same report suggests additional strategies for early literacy: when reading a book with large print, the point at each word as you read it. Your child will understand that the word being spoken is the word she sees

Read a favorite book over and over again.

Read stories with rhyming words and lines that repeat, and have your child join in. Read from a variety of children's books, including fairy tales, poems, and non-fiction.

The more strategies you can incorporate into your child's reading experience, the more likely you are to help your child develop into a strong reader.

RAISING A SUCCESSFUL CHILDREN

The way we praise our children has profound and lasting consequences, yet many parents are doing it wrong.

"Straight As again? You are so smart!" "Look at that drawing. You are such a good artist!"

Many parents assume that it's good to praise children's abilities because it boosts their confidence and self-esteem, which in turn paves the way to success. However, a growing body of research suggests that praising children for their ability destroys their love of learning, their ability to persist in the face of failure, and their chances for success.

Fixed vs. Growth Mindset

To understand how praise can have such negative consequences, you need to understand the work of Carol Dweck. A social psychologist from Stanford University, Dweck has spent most of her research career studying mindsets. She discovered that there are two fundamental mindsets that affect the way you view the world. A fixed mindset is the belief that your qualities, like intelligence and athletic ability, are carved in stone and can't be changed. You're either smart, or you're not. You're either good at sports, or you belong on the sideline. A growth mindset is the belief that your qualities can be cultivated; you can expand your abilities through effort, good strategies, and guidance from others.

The two mindsets affect how people view success and failure. People with a fixed mindset believe that success is due to one's ability, and failure is due to one's lack of ability. As a result, people with a fixed mindset are deflated by failure. They shy away from challenges because they don't want to risk making mistakes and looking bad.

People with a growth mindset attribute failure to a lack of effort or skill – things that can be improved through perseverance. When they fail, they don't view themselves as failures. They believe that mistakes are just problems to be solved.

As you might expect, the mindset has a profound influence on success in school, work, relationships, and many other areas of life.

How Praise Affects Mindset

Praising children's ability reinforces a fixed mindset. When we praise children's ability after they experience success (by telling them they're smart after getting an A on a test, for example), it sends the message that success is due to ability. It also sends the unintentional message that failure is due to lack of ability. This causes children to fear failure and give up when things get tough.

In one classic study, Dweck and her colleague, Claudia Mueller, gave fifth graders a set of moderately difficult questions from an IQ test. All of the children were praised for their performance (which was quite good, overall). Some of them were praised for their intelligence: "Wow…that's a really good score. You must be smart at this." Others were praised for their effort: "Wow…that's a really good score. You must have worked really hard." As expected, children praised for being smartly developed a fixed mindset. When they experienced failure on the second set of very difficult problems, they lost their motivation and did poorly on the third set of easier problems. In contrast, children praised for their effort developed a growth mindset and were persistent in the face of failure. Their motivation and performance didn't suffer.

How to Foster a Growth Mindset

If praising children's abilities is a bad idea, what does a parent have to do? Dweck says that we should use process praise. When children succeed, we should praise the process that led to the success:

"I noticed how hard you studied for your English test. It really paid off!"

"You're finally riding your bike! Way to go! I liked how you picked yourself up after every fall and keep trying until you figured it out."

"That's a beautiful painting. I like how you experimented with different colors."

When children fail, we shouldn't praise their effort as a consolation prize ("You tried your best!"). Instead, we should encourage them to learn and grow from the experience:

"I know you studied hard for that test. Let's see if we can find other study strategies that yield better results."

"You can't paint a masterpiece on your first try. Keep practicing. Every time you paint, you're becoming a better artist."

Failure offers tremendous opportunities for growth. Don't rob your child of those opportunities. Don't be afraid of a little constructive criticism.

What about the kids who do well without even trying? Don't praise them. Instead, encourage them to take on more challenging tasks.

Beware of False Growth Mindset

As the mindset concept gained popularity in parenting and education circles, Dweck noticed that many people have a fundamental misunderstanding of a growth mindset. Many people believe that you should praise children's effort regardless of their performance, but that's wrong. Praising effort is meaningless when children are not doing well.

In the new edition of her book Mindset: The New Psychology of Success, Dweck says that we should praise the learning process that led to the successful outcome, and tie that process to the outcome. The effort is part of the learning process, but it's not the only part. We should acknowledge children's strategies, too. Help them understand how their behavior affected the outcome (e.g., "You tried a lot of different ways of balancing the bike and, because you keep trying, you finally found the right way!"). When children succeed, praise the strategy. When they fail, help them find another strategy.

Dweck concludes that the best way for parents to raise successful children is to teach them "to love challenges, be intrigued by mistakes, enjoy the effort, seek new strategies, and keep on learning."

ABC TO RAISE HAPPY CHILDREN

Wouldn't it be nice to think there was some magic formula for raising happy kids? Some secret way to help your kids have a rocketing self-esteem and wonderful self-worth. The greatest gift a parent can give their kids is a healthy self-esteem. The only problem is you may have no idea where to start. But what if there was a way and it was simpler than you thought?

And that's where the ABC's come in. If you manage to follow these simple concepts you will set your children up with a rock solid foundation for their self-esteem.

A is for appreciating and affirm. Get these two things right and you will notice a huge difference in how your kids interact with you and their peers and most importantly how they feel about themselves. What you appreciate, appreciates and when it comes to your kids there is no difference.

Being a child and a teenager can be a particularly difficult time. They are working out who they are, where they fit in and even if they fit in.

By appreciating and affirming your children, they will realize they are worthy, they are loved and they do belong. They understand they are worthy of being appreciated and affirmed. They understand they are loved and they belong because it is being shown to them by their parents. Your kids may not always demonstrate it but parents love and appreciation is extremely important to them. And if they don't get it from their parents, the effects can be quite detrimental.

It is also important for children to acknowledge what they like and appreciate about themselves. It is one thing for a parent (or someone else) to appreciate them, but the foundations are even more solid when your kids start appreciating themselves. Ask them directly what they like or appreciate about themselves, and don't let them off the hook until they give you an answer!

B is for beliefs. Every single belief we have is made up. And every action we take or don't take is based on the beliefs we have. So doesn't it make sense if our beliefs are made up, we should be making up ones that serve us! You might actually see a stop to self-sabotage.

As parents, we play an important role in the beliefs our children form about life and themselves. Therefore it is imperative we help our kids have beliefs that serve them.

Through our words and actions, we are teaching our kids how they should feel about themselves. The beliefs we have of ourselves as children are the same beliefs we will have as adults. Start telling your kids they are worthy, they are successful, they are perfect the way they are. The sooner they start hearing it, the sooner they will believe it.

C is for consistency. This is often the hardest one for parents and indeed anyone. Life can get in the way. The same way we aren't a parent for just one night, we can't expect to do these things once and never have to do them again. It won't work.

If you are committed to raising happy and confident kids with great self-esteem then you have to be consistent. Every day make a commitment to empowering your kids. Every day make a commitment to tell and show your kids they are loved, they are worthy and they belong. If you make that commitment now not only will they feel great about themselves now, their "armor" will be strong enough as they venture into adulthood.

So remember:

A is for appreciating and affirm

B is for beliefs

C is for consistency

CHAPTER THREE

A Time for Leadership

Breaking a Child's Spirit or Promoting Clear Expectations?

When parents tell me "I don't want to break his (or her) spirit," as an excuse for not wanting to introduce parenting expectations a child might see as negative (like clear boundaries and high expectations), what they are telling me is that they are afraid to lead their children.

Unless parents have clear intentions about what kind of behavior is appropriate and what is not, they develop parent-child relationships that tend to be chaotic and driven by the whims of their kids. They ignore behavior that represents poor judgment, disrespect, impulsivity, and aggression, believing that these negative behaviors are merely a function of "self-expression." As a result, they parent with a blind eye as to how these behaviors shape their children's futures, or worse yet they parent with fear of rejection from their kids, and anxiety, walking on eggshells whenever they want their children to behave.

This can make children feel as though they are the most powerful people in the family, and so kids become insulted when they are not permitted to exercise whatever wish is floating around in their heads (i.e. "I want to eat cookies for breakfast.") You can preserve your child's curiosity, "spirit", independence and personal flair but at the same time you also have to teach your child that

part of their future success will be adjusting to the demands of certain environments where rules and boundaries are important like school, on the playing field and when they are someone else's house.

When you are uncomfortable telling your child to stop talking, be respectful, stop misbehaving, pay more attention, do chores, etc. there are lots of other authority figures who won't hesitate to, and they will often do it without the love and affection you would deliver those messages with. Inevitably parenting criticisms are directed at you when your child ignores the admonitions and you get called up to school for a good talking to. Then the guilt comes, or you might assume the teacher or other significant adult does not really understand your child, or that your child deserves a break at home given the pressure and stress of other environments. Good work habits, respect for others, and self-control all "follow the leader."

PARENTS AS FRIENDS

I have often found it quite ineffective to try to persuade parents to be more strict, expect more from their kids, stick to the consequences they lay out, and incentivize kids without giving them too much "up front," without them earning it. Sometimes, parents tell me, "I don't want my kids to feel the way I did when I was growing up." When parents tell me they don't want to feel the way they did growing up I answer back, "How do you know your kids won't feel worse because you were not the kind of "friend" that they wish you were?" Kids rarely stay close to their childhood friends, but you are a parent forever.

Curiously, when parents if they would like to learn to be better "leaders," and to be able to teach their children the importance of being "successful leaders," almost everyone can listen to that and guide their children through all sorts of challenging life experiences.

The two relationships, friend, and leader are simply not on the same plane.

The basic framework of the parenting education approach I lay out in this ebook is so simple, that even the most anxiety-ridden parent can pull it off. Hopefully, the benefits you reap from this approach will bring you to your next level of evolution, not only as a parent but as a person as well.

Intentions, Actions and Outcomes and the Leadership Framework

The leadership framework I present in this book, revolves around three simple ideas:

- Intentions

- Actions

- Outcomes

After this framework is laid out, you will focus you on how to be an effective motivator, how to communicate effectively and how to help your children understand the relationship between behavior and consequence.

In parenting approach, if you ask parents to think and ask questions:

"What do I want to happen in this interaction with my child?"

What do I have to do to make what I want to happen, actually happen?"

"Did I do it? Did I make it happen? Why? Why not?"

You might be wondering, "Is this really a method? Isn't this what I do all the time, anyway?" I find that most intelligent people ask themselves these questions, but they don't do it enough and they don't do it with purpose, and frequently, they abandon perfectly good parenting strategies because they don't work the first time, or they don't work every time.

I want you to interact with your kids in ways that are purpose-driven and methodical. You, in turn, can teach and share strategies with your partner, and your kids will in turn model this behavior and live their own lives in more purposeful and methodical ways.

IMPROVING YOUR CHILD'S SELF AWARENESS

Self-Awareness is the thinking skill that focuses on a child's ability to accurately judge their own performance and behavior and to respond appropriately to different social situations.

Self-Awareness helps an individual to tune into their feelings, as well as to the behaviors and feelings of others. For example, a child successfully uses self-awareness skills when they notice they are talking too loudly in a library where other children are trying to work, and then adjusts the volume or their voice to a more considerate level. Self-Awareness is vital both to a child's academic success as well as their social and emotional growth. This thinking skill facilitates a child's ability to accurately judge their own performance and behavior, as well as their ability to appropriately respond to different social situations.

As an executive function, self-awareness refers to the capacity to understand the impact of one's behavior on others, as well as the capacity to connect and empathize with individuals in their environments. Self-awareness helps children to be reflective and think about their actions and behavior, as well as to step back and consider what others in their environment are experiencing.

Self-awareness facilitates the capacity to learn from one's mistakes, accept criticism, and listen to and understand the feelings of others. Assessing the executive function of self-awareness in children involves seeing how effectively they understand themselves and others. The Learning-Works for Kids Thinking Skills Assessment is based on the Executive Skills Questionnaire, which measures self-awareness primarily by children's capacity to explain the rationale for their decision making, accurately assess their performance, and their capacity to take on other people's perspectives.

CHAPTER FOUR

RAISING A TEEN MILLIONAIRE

JUST IMAGINE

Take a look at your child or children. What do you imagine they will be doing in the next few years? How do you imagine they'll live their lives when those few years arrive? Imagine that you can have them live that life today and now. If you've thought through in the first paragraph, you may doubt the possibility of your expectation seeing this side of the earth. Most parents may not be able to see their children become today what they naturally expect of them in a few years from now. Our society has taught us that we have to bear the responsibilities of our wards till they are grown before we can empower them. Our brains are wired with the thought that our children are our responsibility so we can bear through with them while we wait for their blossoming into that huge money making a personality that we expect time will make them be.

Now imagine your child runs home, jumps on you and says dad or mom here's what I got $50000, I won the music competition at school. Wouldn't you collect the money, of course, you would? That money is too huge to overlook. You may think that doesn't happen often, but how about if it happens? Our worlds are filled with too many possibilities that our thinking the normal everyday way has overlooked because we think some things are almost impossible that if they happen at all, they happen by chance. We can't imagine a child or even a teen worth a million dollars. The good news is many children your child's age have managed to break of the limitations that their parents placed around them and have gone ahead to do unbelievable things, things their parents could never have done at their age. Some parents who had the same information as I am about sharing with you in this book have helped position their children and are benefitting from the wealth they have helped their children create.

I am not talking about abusing a child by asking the child to go work at a tender age to care for himself. No, I am talking about helping your child discover the hidden capacities in him that can make him sell out. If your child gets to know what the richest men in the world know at their tender age, you will be positioning them with the right information. Information is empowerment.

Once they are informed and guided as they will easily accept, you will be creating a giant of your child in no time. The late Michael Jackson's father Joseph Jackson will be a good tutor in this regard. He discovered talent and capacity in his wards and went ahead to develop that talent that became the cynosure of global eyes. Michael Jackson from his teenage age was making more in one night than what many parents in his time earned joined together. When Joseph Jackson began putting his ward through, his wards too might have assumed that dad was having them go through rigorous work and that they were way too little. He never looked away from this training because he acknowledged that in his wards was a capacity that could make them stand-out and etch a living. He first saw the genius in Michael.

If you look straight into your wards, you'd find that incredible talent that often you overlook. You know your child can write, sing, draw or is good at some great deal but you push the development of that part of your child to the teachers at school who may not recognize those talents. You failed your child. You have to do more; you have to take over the responsibility of building your child's talent.

Musical icons such as Justin Bieber started way early and were already renowned for their talents before they were even teenagers. Of course, with renown arrives wealth. If you start this early, before long, your child will be celebrated. And guess what? The earlier your child discovers he is very good at doing what he does; you create a launch pad for the full maximization of his talents when he finally reaches the age of independence.

Now imagine, what is it your child loves doing and you know he has shown the capacity to do well? Think on this. Imagine your child at what you have observed he loves doing and sees him in an atmosphere where he can do what he does and be celebrated.

If you can picture it, that's actually where your child should be. The question you will be asking yourself is "what is it I must do to bring out the best with a commercial value in my child. Think. If you can think, before long the answers will arrive and when they do, you act in that direction. Your child may not be able to think for himself now so all the propulsion to succeed will be dependent on you. All the ethics that he has to apply will depend on your ethics. If you turn out a bad timekeeper, he'd certainly walk in your footsteps. You must know in advance where your child is going and equip yourself with all the necessary tools like this book.

Your child is that genius whose time has arrived. He will sure be proud of a father or mother who is helping position him where he could never have being. Imagine you are the father of a twelve-year-old millionaire. It's not impossible. If you can think it, you can do it.

KNOW YOUR CHILD

Today's parents are often way too busy to have time for their wards. They are always everywhere and suddenly they discover they are nowhere around their wards. Most parents come to this knowledge after time has gone and it hits them how fast their wards have grown ahead of them and they have failed to be part of their children's growing up years. These parents have left all the development of their wards to the teachers at school and friends.

Teachers could be very good at what they do but they can never be as good as you to your child. God could have handed your wards at birth to the teacher, not you but he believed in your capacity to build your child. If you are thinking you've sent your child to the best school in town and that's what every great father is doing, you've got it all wrong. You remain the greatest adventurer to the unknown world of your child's future, the successful/millionaire future.

How much of your child do you know? Sadly, many a parent would find this answer unanswerable. They are way too far their wards and their wards are wishing they could have just a bit of them. You can't want to get the best out of something if you don't know the workings of that thing. You can't get the best of your child if you don't know your child. You have to know your child's weaknesses, strengths, likes, dislikes, chores etc. this helps you build them around their strengths and also see how to develop their weaknesses.

Now that you are reading this book and thinking of how to make your child a millionaire before he turns twenty, you'd be tweaking your mind on where and how you must direct your energy around your child that you know very well to make the most of his strength and weaknesses. In the previous part, I said that the millionaire is in your child's talent. Many parents think that the son of the other guy is quite good at what he does and has become famous so my child will have to follow his footsteps. You are not trying to become Mr. Joseph Jackson. Not everyone will be lucky to produce a child protégé as Michael Jackson was. So you trying to develop your child into another Michael Jackson will be another mistake if your child has no singing or dancing talents.

Your child's talent like your talent is where the millionaire treasures of this world lay. You have to know your child's talents and capabilities and then you look for means to develop that talent into marketable value. If your child has craved for drawing and painting, don't try to make him a singer because you think singers make a hell lot of money. Many singers don't. If your child is good at athletics don't think he is wasting his energy because you think he should be better playing the keyboard. Flow with what your child likes best. So if you have no idea what your child loves to do then, you really don't know your child.

The question of whether you really know your child may pop right into your brains. It's understandable. Ask yourself how best you know your child better than your neighbors and friends know. For many parents, friends and neighbor seem to know better than them who their children really are. As a parent, you are not just your child's father or mother. You are a mentor and a guide. Get it. Your neighbors and friends can't go the extra mile. They may discover your child's ability and they'd say nothing about it. Those who are good enough will tell you your child is incredibly talented but will stop just there. They won't seek to help your child expand into the realities that could happen with such incredible talent. If you, therefore, fail to know your child and his capabilities you will be far away from making millions yourself.

Now, look at your child. What do you see? Do you see a successful millionaire? This may still be very difficult a question to answer even if you think you know your child's enormous capacities. There may be the fear that your child may not flow in the direction of your desire to align his attributes with making money. It's normal if this happens. At least you have taken the first step of studying your child and discovering his hidden potentials. You have passed your first test. The next will take a natural course. This natural course may involve your trying to convince your child about his abilities even if that child doesn't think his abilities are not worth looking at.

Maybe your child may have this skills that you've discovered he has but he has no idea he even has them or that they are as valuable as you or others may be thinking they are. You will have to help your child discover himself. You discover him first and then you help him discover what lies in that potential that you think he has.

If your child already knows he has great potentials at what he loves to do, it makes the job easy for you. You both know the potential is there and he will be readily available to tow your line of thought of trying to help him make the best of his talents for himself.

But now first lets imagine you've discovered some hidden talent in your child that your child is shy to act on or let's say a friend has whispered in your ears that your child has tremendous talents at something that you can make the best of but your child doesn't know or isn't ready to talk about it. The next chapter will help you help your child discover what his potential that you have seen in him.

KNOW YOUR CHILD'S LEARNING STYLE

If you want to be an effective homeschooler, you must know your child's learning style. What is her preferred method for grasping information? Most people use a combination of styles but have a decided predilection for one. There are three basic learning styles: auditory, visual, and kinesthetic or physical. Adjusting your style of teaching to her style of learning will greatly enhance the homeschooling experience for both of you. So, let's explore these styles.

An auditory learner is one who learns best by hearing. She does well in a lecture class or by listening to audiobooks. It is not unusual to hear her repeating something out loud when she is trying to memorize the information. This type of learner is usually good at linguistics. She picks up foreign languages easily, and when speaking with people who have accents, she may subconsciously begin speaking with that accent. My wife has to warn our foreign friends that my daughter and I are not trying to mimic them. We can't help ourselves. Some auditory learners insist on having music in the background while they are studying. It helps them focus. Ironically, others demand complete quiet. Any sound that does not pertain to what they are studying is a distraction. Does your child frequently break out in the song? Does she make up a melody in order to memorize a poem? When the light bulb turns on in her head, does she say, "I hear what you mean."? If so, she is probably an auditory learner.

A visual learner is easier to recognize. She prefers reading over being read to. You will often find her drawing or coloring. List making and doodling are common pastimes. It will take her awhile to understand a lecture, so putting an outline or notes on the board would be a great help to her. Try to avoid oral testing. She will do better with writing essays or drawing maps. She will be a meticulous note taker. Her notes will be complete with underlining, color coding, charts, and diagrams. Do not be surprised when you discover her fashion consciousness. This applies to boys, too. If you have more than one child, the quiet one is more likely to be a visual learner. Her light bulb response would be, "I see where you are coming from."

Kinesthetic learning, or learning by doing, is the most prominent style found in young children. This is due in part to their lack of development. As your children grow, the one that cannot sit still is the kinesthetic learner. She has to experience things and will be bored to death by lectures. She will be your athletic child, always on the go. Spelling and handwriting - forget about it. Give her a nice lab course any day. She will prefer adventure books and movies over the classics. Having her build a diorama depicting a scene from a book will benefit her more than writing a book report. Field trips are one of your best tools for teaching your kinesthetic learner. Most importantly, allow her to move around, and give her breaks throughout the day. With our son, we would occasionally stop lessons and go to the park for an hour to let him burn off some of his never-ending energy. Lightbulb moment: "I'm getting a handle on this subject."

It is easy to see the usefulness of adapting your teaching to the child's style of learning. To not do so would result in a long, difficult, and frustrating school year. You will actually find it refreshing to be able to use different teaching methods for each of your children. It will eliminate monotony. Have fun, and enjoy your kids!

CHAPTER FIVE

GUIDING YOUR CHILD TO DISCOVER HIS TALENTS

Great parents want the best for their children. I've said before that we often pray for a bright future as parents of our children. We hope our children's future is bright i.e. future. We fail to look at the present and how bright we can make the present be. A father will tell his child, I'm doing this so that you can have the best of tomorrow. What your child actually wants is tomorrow today. Your child already knows what the big lifestyle of the very rich are; posh cars, a home in a posh suburb, and lots of money. They know. At a tender age, the television and movies have done all the spoiling that our children no longer dream of the future.

The future is the future. They'd like to live in the present realities of what they can do now. At tender age children and teens begin to copy musical icons and other famous acts. They want to sing, be famous and very rich. Your child wants to be very rich. Parents have been to reserving at talking about money to their wards. Seriously, they think their children aren't worth understanding how money works at this tender age so they let go that topic for the future when the rat race begins to catch with them. No better time there is to talk about money and developing their talents and capacity than now when they are not yet caught in the web of rats. It will be a pleasurable ride and the benefits are huge. If your child understands the money principle early on say at ten before they are fifteen they'd be successful millionaires already.

If your child's above ten, you are still on course to having a successful millionaire teen or early ties before five years elapses. Let's say you've discovered by careful study of your child that he has a special talent that you think is worth developing, something he really loves but your child has no idea what he loves doing has huge potentials for him to make money and fame from it. You will have to talk to him about it.

THIS "TALK" WILL INVOLVE:

Talent

Tell him you know he is a very talented guy and superstar even if he hasn't gotten there yet. Create for his images of successful people who equally had the talents like he has. Let him know you know he is equally as talented as the other guys and that where those other celebrated guys are is where he should be and that you are in the position and very able to drive him there.

Attitude

Tell him he will have developed the same attitude as those talented guys. They've got great attitude so he has to develop their same attitude. The successful guys are often determined, hardworking and persevering, the same attitude he would have to develop very early when there is really no pressure to succeed.

Lucre

Money speaks and he has to know that. Of course, he may know how important money is to the day to day running of the family but beyond he must know money as a source of power, fame and more wealth.

Knowledge

There are many people who are equally as talented as the guy who is celebrated. It is what they know beyond their talent. Talent speaks but knowledge does more, it walks. Let him know he may be talented but he will do better with the knowledge you are offering him, a bigger experience of many years of your failures and weakness and your perseverance to see he doesn't make the same mistakes as you have made. Yes, you've made mistakes.

The talk you are offering your child is a priceless bait. Often your child realizes this early at a tender age after your reassurances of a better future applying what he has gotten inside him. He will certainly enjoy the company of his father or mother who believes he has potentials and is ready to help him strive towards accomplishing that potential.

Venus and Serena Williams's world tennis champions and one-time number one and two interchangeably were propelled into becoming champions by their dad who saw the massive talents in his arsenal and decided he would get the best out of them. Venus and Serena have been a delight to watch too many tennis fans and a motivation to non-tennis fans. You can take Mr. Williams for motivation. Mr. Williams might never have to be a local championship winner but he won all there is to be won in tennis with his two daughters.

Don't think you aren't even qualified because your child hasn't seen you succeed in a business or that task that you want him to do. You are the strongest motivation for your child and if you say go especially at that tender age when he believes you absolutely, he will learn to believe you throughout his life. If you could not do it, maybe it's because you never had the motivation. Your child can when you motivate him to see the realities of what he has up there.

Today's children know money. What they don't know is that they can make that money before they grow into becoming adults. Money could be the strongest attraction and when you are around that, they could be confident around you. When you talk your child into seeing his potentials and how he can make the best of him, you will constantly have to do the guidance. You'd be like a coach to your child. He may not read all the books there is to read but you must read them for him. He may not have all the money to invest in his skill initially; you will have to invest that money.

Money is only gotten from money

You don't have to cuddle him. It isn't necessary. All you have to do is give him the air to breathe. Let the idea of him developing his talents look like he is the owner even when you are the person instigating it. Children easily let go and become tired when they are being forced to take an action. Inspire and motivate him. That's all he needs once he discovers he has the capacity. It's very important your child knows that he has the capacity and talents to be like some of the other celebrated millionaires. If you can help him think it, he could as well do it.

How about if you think your child is untalented and that you've not seen anything too special that is worth developing as per skill. The next chapter is talking about helping your seemingly untalented child find a talent that he can develop and be very good at to become successful.

HELPING YOUR CHILD DEVELOP THEIR TALENTS

It may not be immediately apparent, but all children are very good at

SOMETHING. In the modern education process, these God-given strengths and talents are often overlooked. Identifying these special talents is an integral aspect of child development. If your child has a special talent, his or her schoolteachers should know of it - it may not always translate into better grades, but it will definitely help in bringing out your child's special persona.

A child's special talents can be overlooked in school for various reasons. For instance, he or she may not speak English as a primary language. In many cases, a talented child is sensitive to the point of introversion, in which case his or her special abilities are hidden under a bushel for the most part of the school years. If your child attends a school that, apart from academics, also focuses on identifying children's special abilities, your child is indeed lucky. Such schools usually have methods of grooming such gifts and helping the child develop them.

However, it all begins with you - the parent. There is really no substitute for helping your kid to develop his or her special ability at home. It is only when you have identified such a talent and pointed it out to your child convincingly that you should make the school aware of it. This cannot be early enough, and it doesn't require you to have that talent yourself - or even a lot of money to spare for the grooming process. All you really need to do is encourage your child to set higher goals for himself in that department. He needs to know that he can succeed in it if he applies himself sufficiently.

The will to pursue and polish any talent begins with an appreciation for it from those who matter in our lives. You, as parents, are the most significant and influential people in your child's life. Your appreciation and encouragement will set the cornerstone for his willingness to develop a talent for music, painting, writing, public speaking, sports, etc.

Also, expose your child to notable personalities who have this talent. For example, if your child has a special ability for playing the flute, make him watch videos of famous flutists. This will help him find a role model to emulate - even a genius child learns mostly by imitation to begin with. Once you have laid the groundwork for your child's growth in this field, alert his school and enlist his teachers' cooperation in grooming it further. In many schools, children earn extra credits by participating in cultural events, so it may make a difference in your child's grades even if his or her talent has no immediately apparent academic value. Most importantly, however, you are helping your child become a unique individual.

I've heard a couple of parents complain about their children's inability. They'd often tell me they've done all there is they can do for their child and they've not seen any improvements. I've often told them to relax. Every child is a talent and there is a box of skills available in your child that perhaps you have failed to allow strive.

Some parents often try to compare their children with the children of their friends. I've often said that there is no comparison we can use to compare any child. Every child is unique in some great way that we can never be correct thinking the other child is far way better than this one. If you think your child isn't talented or as talented as the other children around, it means you have quite a lot of work to do. Maybe you've not created the right atmosphere for the talent of your child to strive. It's either you are doing too little or too much and either way kills the soup. There must be the right balance of everything and finding that right balance is where most parents get it wrong.

We often feel as parents that it is in our place to ensure our wards get off to the best start in getting them moving as fast as we wish. We fail to look and consider the child's strengths and weakness in relation to our goals. We tend to force talents on our children rather than making them discover and grow with what they have discovered about themselves. Most parents have defined professions for their wards before they even begin to get into school and they force their wards through their own training directed towards their chosen profession while their wards struggle to accomplish their parents wish. While many children have managed to get through with their parents' wishes, most have hit a strong rock. The result is a battered future, what their parents had not anticipated.

What you need do is to leave your child with all the air he needs to breath. Let him learn to discover himself without you. Don't try to poke into his affairs. He may just be too shy to act around you. Pretend you aren't around and you don't mind him especially when he is around his peers. Watch. Children often become their best when they are around other children.

Sometimes we raise our children in grown-up environments and expect them to level up with our thinking and philosophy at their tender age. Children will be children and you can't help it. If you force their development, you will be endangering them. What I mean is that you will make a millionaire out of your child without much stress when he learns to find in himself his own capacity that he finds joy doing and then you adapt it as his selling strength.

Some children tend to do more alone. That's where they often find the right inspiration to be their best so being around you may hinder their creativity. Discover if your child is this type and help him make good use of this quality. Some parents scare their children off from a tender age that when the children grow up they push themselves away from their parents. This set of parents may not see anything special about their kids. It pays to attract your children towards you even if he is worthless. He could be worth so much with warmth from you.

Children naturally love to share what they can do with everyone who cares about how they feel and shows some good interest in them, a good reason for you to also show real interest in your child, how they relate, what they do, how they think, why they think the way they do, and where they'd like to be now and in the immediate future.

Try to think how your child thinks. Before long, you will discover that that child of yours who capacity you overlooked was worth more than gold. Think like Abraham Lincoln whose unwavering faith in his son prompted his letter of confidence. Do everything you can and everything you should do to ensure your child becomes the superstar. If you cannot help him move gear at what he loves doing, you cannot help him make money this early. Once you've helped your child recognize himself, you will need to teach him about money.

Teach Your Child Money Management

You might have grown up in an environment where understanding money and loving money by children was considered inappropriate. I grew up in such environments. If a child loved money or had a clinging for it, our elders concluded that before long that child will go stealing to get it so they kept the understanding and loving of money from us for as long as they could. But somehow, we had to use money and we learned to use money even for inappropriate things. I thought, Wouldn't it have great we learned very early how best to use the money to make the best of our lives? It will shock you what I'm about asking you to do.

You will have to trade off those old set of beliefs and pick up this one, that your child must understand how money works and how it is gotten so that he understands how best to use it for maximum benefits for you and for himself. Children learn to spend. We give them quite a lot as daily stipends for their sweets and burger. Because you've told them to buy for themselves that sweet thing, they naturally assume that every money that steps into their hand is for buying sweets and biscuits.

Only a handful of children think they can save some of their money and the reason for saving is to buy something bigger in the future that the little everyday money would not get in one go. Our society has helped us mold our children with the buying mentality. If a child is asked "what do we use the money for?" the answer that pops from his mouth is, "for buying what we want." Its buy, buy, buy. But you see, that's the difference between the children who become millionaires early in their lives. These children have been tutored on savings and applying money to make more money. Yes, a child may have talent, but that talent will require some money to bring it to valuable form where more money can be made. Children who have gone ahead to make millions early in their lives learn to save.

Many parents often collect money given to their wards by family members or acquaintances in the name of saving it for their wards and they end up using the money at the end. When the child asks for the money, parents often ask the child where the money for the food comes from. If you've been acting this way, you've not been helping your child develop the financial lifestyle that could help him become financially knowledgeable.

At some point as your child grows, you will have to teach him confidence in himself to handle money. My dad used to hand over his salary to me to help him count. He even showed me where he kept the money in the house and asked me sometimes to help him get it. I understood that he was developing trust in me and that experience has helped me tremendously as a grown up.

Teach your child to trust in his capacity to keep money by allowing him to keep his money by himself under your supervision. Once in a while, you can ask him how much he has in his accounts and gives him a pat on his back for saving the much he has saved. It's a morale booster for him to save more and to develop a freer air when it comes to dealing with money with you.

Today's banking world has opened opportunities for kids to save. Gone are those days when a person has to be eighteen before he is entitled to an account. This day even babies own accounts. Teach your child the usefulness of banks. Take him one more step better than his teachers in school by opening a bank account and helping him save what he has been able to save in the house in the bank. Let him also learn to see his account grow fat by his own little inputs. It's a necessary knowledge boost as it helps your child know the value of saving money having money early in life.

Money doesn't answer all that one needs. You should know that and let your kids know same. Money isn't everything and having more money doesn't guarantee you peace of mind. The reason our society has a lot of juveniles who are getting locked up in our nation's penitentiaries is that these young men and women were untutored on the money.

They push for money ahead of anything and would kill or maim to get it and then accept the risk of years in the prison for just a stint of money. This excuse has always been the reason many parents refuse to teach their children about money so early so that they don't end up as rogues searching for it. Your child deserves to know getting money is not the altruistic source of comfort but just a means to an end that comfort only arrives when we are able to align our money need in relation to solving problems that supply us with joy.

Our relationship with others should not be encumbered by the amount of money we have garnered. Rather, it should help us develop that relationship. If it doesn't, you are way far from enjoying your wealth. Children may fall prey to the temptation of becoming callous or proud because they feel their parents are well to do. A child who understands money will do otherwise. He will understand that money comes and goes but what stays with us are the relationships we've been able to garner, these relationships worth so much more. Money should help us create relationships not destroy them.

The common saying that money is a necessary evil may be correct. I'd redefine that statement for your child as "understanding money early in life is a necessary evil." We don't get money by pursuing money; we get money by pursuing joy, happiness, peace, satisfaction, and contentment. If one pursues money, he will end up having money rule him. If one pursues a healthy relationship with joy, happiness, peace etc., money runs after him as a tool to bolster these relationships. The earlier your child understands money, the better for you. Your child's understanding of how money works could be the inertia for getting and benefitting from that money that he gets.

How Money Works

You are in a position to tutor your child on how money works because he has to learn from you first. You may not be a businessman but it is still expected that you answer this basic money question. You have to show them how it works. Let's say your child runs up to you and says dad or mom, how does money work for us? I'd really like to know. You might first of all look up at the ceiling and think about what you would answer. You may find yourself giving the same answer as their teachers would often tell them at school. The teachers at school don't know money beyond the wages they collect at the end of the week or month.

Your child deserves more. Even if you are not a businessman, you must be convincing enough to let him know what he has to know that will position him. Money doesn't work in the bank though you may have profits given from the bank as interest from your savings. Teaching your child to save as explain in a previously was only as a means to help him learn the value of having some money that he can call him and can be proud about. But don't teach him money grows in the bank. You sure know that money doesn't grow there. Money grows where it works that is at businesses that people put their energy and talents to develop.

At some point, as you watch your child's bank account grow bigger, you may have to whisper in his ears that he would have to invest his money. This investment at least at that early time should be creative i.e. something he can visualize and see that he loves to do. If your child likes to sing, you may as well help him with developing a soundtrack. Let him know his little savings helped him accomplish that even if you had to do most of the work for him. By that, you will be helping him see money beyond the usual burger and sweets.

The only way money works are by allowing it work. It seems common sense but it's not easy a task to get that done. The reason is that we often have numerous needs that overwhelm the amount of money at our disposal. One fact is, money can never be enough. We can never be satisfied with the amount of money we have. This is one truth your child will soon come to experience as he grows however if he understands this early the better for him. This will help him beat a better standing especially now that he has less to worry about and you are doing all the worrying.

Money has the power to persuade. It's an incredibly powerful persuasion tool that is capable of changing one's demeanor towards you once it stands on the table. Your child may not be aware of this at his early age but he will certainly come to terms with this and may be in the right knowledge to use it to get the kind of following that he desires. Yes, relationships may come first but when you require people to get a task done even beyond their will, some notes of money may come handy. The amount of money put into a project will determine the proportionate increased amount that will return. If money doesn't live your hands, it's not going to return and it wouldn't be useful. Money finds value when an action is carried out with it. If you put so little amount of it, so the little effect will be felt. If you want to develop your child's talent, for example, you'd have to bury yourself in books that may cost so much and you have to invest into your child's talent by having him go for training from the most reputable trainers to put finishing touches to that talent.

All these will cost money. Before your child becomes that finished product with the expected millions he'd be making, so much had gone into developing him however talented he may seem. Your child must realize this early that though he may have talent, his talent isn't just enough. The talent must be financed and developed to the state of acclaim. Money thus will be seen as a tool for developing talent from that early age. The more money and time he puts into developing his talent the more better he becomes. Now that you know how money works, you may be wondering if you really can raise the amount of money to create the best of your child's talent.

How to Keep Your Child Focused On the Development Process

It's not easy to get a child to do something day in day out in the name of making millions. Already you know how difficult making your child understand what you intend to make of him has been. Even more difficult will be the training process and the ability for him to sit and get through the classes or the training that will be involved. The key word your child has to learn is the focus. He needs to focus and you have to be the one to help him focus.

Children can be forgetful and you as a parent must be the timekeeper. You don't expect your child to keep to time every time that's why they have you to help. Every time you will have to be on the watch and remind him when he has to go to practice classes. If possible, you can decide to take the position as a driver to drop him at the class as much as you can especially at the beginning. You have to persistently place the big picture you desire before him. Help him with pictures of his models as much as you can. Ask him who his models are. Chance is he would have models around the skills or talents he likes. Let those models are the big picture and if possible, act as you are also a big fan of his models. This will keep him focused especially as he knows you would like to idolize him like you do his idols.

Children's minds change very often and they easily find new things they like if the former things are no longer attractive. It will be your duty to keep the things you think he is presently focused on as beautiful so that he can continuously look at developing himself in that direction. Children tend to give up easily if they try and fail as often and they love to be consoled as often when they fail. You have to console him anytime you observe he is going through the downside of life. It helps to build the courage to help him start over and over again even if he fails. One may have talent and great talent at that and still fail to meet up with challenges.

Challenges are not overcome by talent; they are overcome by perseverance and persistence. If your child will have to win through with his talents, he must develop a fighting will and a persistence to win even if he is failing. These are attributes you have to teach him.

If you truly want to make the best of your child, you will have to develop; a fighting will yourself and teach him to also fight hard. Those who win are those who can fight hard however terrible the battle becomes. When you develop a fighting zest, your child takes after you. He will do as you do.

An outstanding passion. What stands successful persons out is passion. Those who are passionate enough do great things actually do great things. If you are passionate enough about your goal for your child, your child will certainly develop into an outstanding act too.

A courageous stance. It's difficult when one has to face challenges that are sometimes bigger than expected. Your goal is certainly big and that's why you need courage. It's not going to be the normal everyday race. There will be bumps and gullies but you have determined to run and not just run but win and so you must. An understanding mane. To be focused on anything, it means you have grappled with the complexities of that thing and appreciated or understood the requirements expected of it. It's not an easy virtue understanding but when reaching towards a complex goal as making your child a millionaire, you will have to understand the complexities of the task and take your time to appreciate what's underneath.

A systemic approach to solving problems that arrive. There certainly will be challenges on the way to attaining your goals. The difference will be that you have prepared for that challenge by developing an approach. Problems can be resolved by taking decisive steps against them. The making of a child millionaire isn't always an easy road. All those child superstars that you are familiar with were the handiwork of their parents focus on helping their children focus on becoming the big name that they have turned out to be. If you truly think your child deserves that superstar child millionaire status, you will face your task squarely with all the energy you can garner and then put your child together to see through your own lens too.

Don't think what you will be doing for your child is too difficult a task. Just think it and focus on what you think. You will be done in no time. You've seen the need for focus in this part. No great achievement comes without a persistent focus on the achievement prior to achieving it. If you think making your child a millionaire is an achievement worth getting, just go ahead and pursue with all the focus you can garner. You will get it.

The next challenge will be to help your child develop the right goals once he has set his mind towards developing his talents and capacities. Every person has to focus on something worthwhile. We don't just focus on our talents and skills; our focus has to be goal oriented.

TEACH YOUR CHILD TO SET ACHIEVABLE GOALS FROM CHILDHOOD

One of the greatest challenges being faced by many persons is the problem of setting goals. As your child learns to grow under your tutelage, focusing on becoming better at what he or she already thinks he knows best, he may have vague images of what he has to pursue. Yes, he knows he has to improve that's why you are helping him and he hopes to make some millions out of his talent as you may assure him but he has no knowledge that those goals are actually the ultimate. He'd have to learn to set short-term goals first as a preview of the long-term goals.

Your child's goals could be well defined if you have the goals yourself. Children may enjoy winning but they have to be motivated towards the challenges that winning arrives from. You will have to understand that though you may have the big picture which you believe your child is capable of attaining, little challenges will have to be overcome en-route to the big challenge.

If your child is talented at playing football, and you are developing him through a youth team of a local side, you will first have him strive to outdo his teammates and make the first team as much as he can and then score goals as often as he can. You can begin to set a benchmark of goals he should say in a season while you find it possible always to stand in the stands and watch him play. I used football here but it could go for any talent. Let your child find pleasure in knowing he is as good as you claim by motivating him to make short-term goals of outdoing those around him. The more short-term success he achieves, the more his gaze widens towards the possibilities of the long term that you are hoping he reaches.

Deliberately slide your goals and watch him act around it. Inspire and motivate him with words like "your hero started like this." If there are autobiography videos of his superstar icons, you can help him with them and join his watch. All superstars had to go through the same process he will have to go through. The difference was the attitude they each had.

Even if your child doesn't hit the initial goals, that doesn't mean he is way far from the future goal. Don't hit him and say, you aren't impressive or you are wasting my time and energy. Statements like that can lower morale and diminish any passion that had existed in the child. If he failed to meet the initial goal, it only helps you see where he isn't doing well and then help him focus on developing those grey areas.

Don't write your child's future prospects off because of today's mediocre achievements. Many of those child icons celebrated today were a result of continuous persistence at developing them by their parent's or guardians. They often had to fail not to hit their initial targets many times but they learned to perfect it and got going.

Don't want to hit your child with becoming the best immediately like some persons do. Some parents will say; that's not the way Michael Jordan bounces the basketball, if you must be like him, you must do it like him. They forget that Michael Jordan developed his great skill over time. Jordan was talented from his youth but he wasn't skillful. Skill comes with practice and learning. Yes, we want our children to quickly attain the pace of Bolt, or the dribbling skills of Messi but these persons didn't attain that pace or skill when they were little. They learned with experience.

Your child's dramatic talent is dramatic enough to bring him into the limelight but if he has to be extraordinary, he will have to prove himself overtime at the development table. You'd have to allow him to learn how best he has applied his skills to enable him to create that difference that can only be his. Talking about skills and talent, some persons may assume that they are one and the same. Well, they are both different.

UNDERSTANDING THE DIFFERENT BETWEEN YOUR CHILD'S SKILL AND TALENT

We often do not know the difference between skill and talent, I mean most persons. We often make the general assumption that a person who has talents has developed skill.It's not always the case and you will come to discover in your child how far your child's talents are different from the skills that he will require to accomplish the great feet you are envisioning his talents has the capacity for.

The innate capacity of your child that he finds ease with is his talent. I've written before that everyone has some incredible talent and these talents are the difference makers in a man's life. A man who will find his talents and develop them will be privileged to eat the fruits of such talents. The fact that one has talent and knows the capacity of the talent doesn't, however, mean he will tap all the gold out of it. You might have had the situation of a person who is so knowledgeable at what he does yet doesn't make headway. One could be so good. Being so good at doing something is talent. Applying what you are good at to make progress in life is a skill.

Are there not many talented footballers out there? Of course, there are, but that doesn't guarantee that they would all make the number one spot in their career lifetime. That's the skill difference. Those who make the world footballers of the year every year aren't often the most talented players on the planet. They are only those who are able to apply their talent with skill.

A major difference between these two is that talent is innate, skill is learned. Skill qualifies talent. Skill is the action one takes at developing talent. Why I have to differentiate this is because some person may think that immediately one discovers a talent, he could just immediately begin to expect some money. It doesn't work that way. You will have to perfect the talent by developing and applying the skill. If you truly want to get the best out of your child's talent, you will have to learn to help him discover his how to develop skill around what he has talent at.

So many persons are basketball talents playing in the NBA but Michael made a clear mark because he found skill around his basket-balling talent that made him incredibly better than other even better talents. It's about skill. Footballers are talents and they pass the ball the same way. The difference amongst footballers is the skills of each player; the dribbling skills, free-kick skills, spot-kicks skills etc., which they often have to develop individually. Some players' hire personal coaches to help them develop the skills they think they need.

If you truly want your child to discover who and what he really is, you will have to help him with developing certain skills that can stand his talent out. What stands a talent out is the skill. Everyone can sing but Michael Jackson will be Michael Jackson any day because of the skill with which he sang. That skill stood him out. You have to discover the salient parts of your child's talents that you know he has to develop. Skill doesn't come over a nights practice. It will take some time to create that uniqueness that you really want for your child. That time may be two weeks or as long as five years and it will cost as much or so little.

It's true that talent could be very remarkable but skill makes you extraordinary. Skill creates that godlike aura, the reason why superstars are superstars. Superstars have talent mixed with skill. Every child has that craving to be superstars and you'd discover your children crave if you watch him closely. Your child may even begin to try out his model's skills in a bid to be like him. At this time you'd wish for an originality that is distinct and that's where you have to work out the distinctness.

That originality that you want is only developed when you help him mix skill and talent. You do not want a copy but an original empowered by creativity. Developing skill could be expensive. The more expensive a skill, the more valuable it is nothing is really too much to offer if your child will have to perfect that little part of his talent to enable him to stand out. Don't feel shy about spending well if you have to. The more you spend, the more your chances of getting your child become better faster and soonest too, the millionaire status. The difference is clear, talent is inborn, and skill is learned. Skilled learned to develop talent makes you even better at what you do.

CHAPTER SIX

CREATE THAT ORIGINALITY FOR YOUR CHILD AWAY FROM YOUR CHILD'S MODEL

One of the ways you are able to decipher what talent your child has is to look at those persons that he tries to model. You will observe that your child somehow tries to do it like the other renowned guy out there. It's a great virtue but that won't create the individual originality that you want your child to have. Being original stands you out and your child's originality will surely stand him out from the crowd. What you want is a standout. Those that end up making the millions and billions are only a few and a long length apart from those who don't who are the majority of people.

Everyone tries to copy or be like but just a few think they can take the initiative of defining where they stand amongst a crowd of similarly talented persons. Tailors are excellently talented at what they do. But you would often observe that tailors find a way around their talent by creating designs that are original. The reason is that their creativity defines their style and how rated they get to become over time. The tailor who doesn't create his own style only joins the crowd of tailors without labels. The one who creates gets labeled. The difference is often clear. The labeled tailor will earn more for his work and have less to prove because every mistake becomes a style while unlabeled will try to prove he is worth it by trying to design masterpieces of the labeled designer.

We don't want to think that our children's talent is meant for the crowd. We know it has stood out capacity. We'd be grooming their minds to think outside the normal box and recreate the originality that characterizes them. Being original doesn't mean you might not have copied some person. You could copy and still be original. That's what is called rebranding in business terms. Nothing is original as long as we find ourselves on this side of the world. What however changes is the quality we add to that already existing principle. That's where the value lies.

Our ability to get the best out of an already existing object is often where creativity and originality lies. Everyone runs, but who runs faster makes the difference. It is guaranteed that anyone who wants to get ahead of the crowd must, by all means, do something about what the crowd is doing and find some way to get it done in a more elegant fashion.

Being original actually means being creative in doing what is normal. You are not going to do anything new. Everything that has to be done has been done already. All that remains is the style with which these things will be done; faster or smarter. Help your child find his originality by helping him become increasingly more creative.